P.S.

The songs of William Michael Perry and Gary William Steaggles

Perrysongs Music Publishing Ltd
Marendellas Drive, Auckland 2014 NZ

This book contains songs written by W.M. Perry and G.W. Steaggles. International copyright secured. Copyright exists in all compositions. Unauthorized copying, arranging, adapting, recording or public performance is an infringement of copyright. All Rights Reserved.

Published by Perrysongs Music Publishing Ltd (New Zealand)
First published 2021
ISBN : 978-0-473-56276-2
All Rights Reserved
Printed in USA

Acknowledgements; Special thanks to Nick Jones at Nick Jones Music for his assistance in scoring this material.

Contents

21 Abingdon Court - 5

Blonde Streaks - 10

Blue Continent - 14

Close Encounters - 17

Close To Home - 21

Coloured Paper - 25

Double Dutch - 29

Factory Madness - 33

Family - 36

Jehovah's My Witness - 41

Klutz And Co - 45

Lover Cover Girl - 48

Mr Valentine - 51

Occupational Hazards - 54

Only When You Laugh - 57

Pink Balloons And Frozen Food - 60

Policeman's Daughter - 65

Spy - 68

Take My Wife - 70

This Is My Night - 75

Photo : Bob Eaton

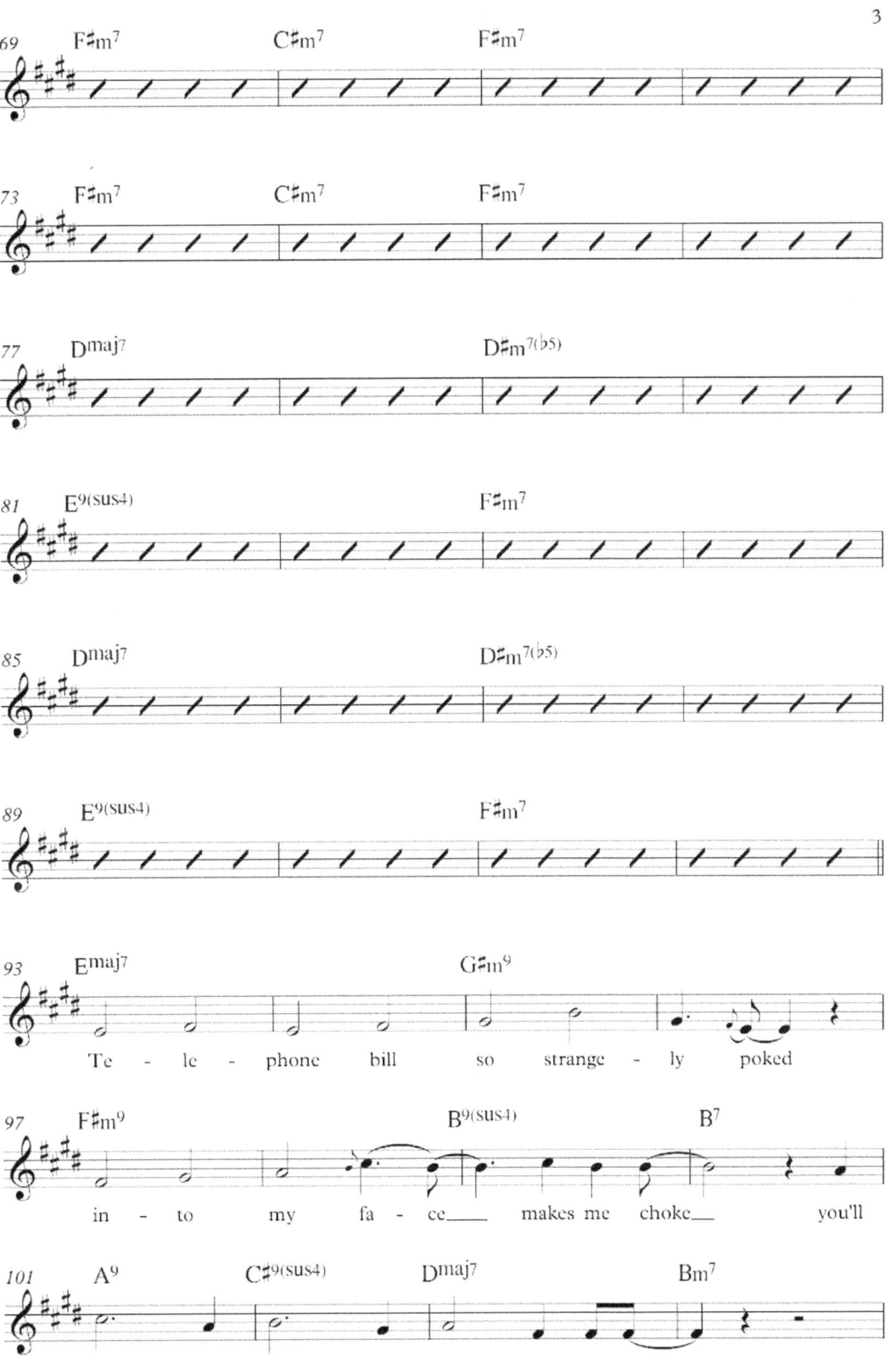

Blue Continent

Words & Music by
B. Perry & G. Steaggles

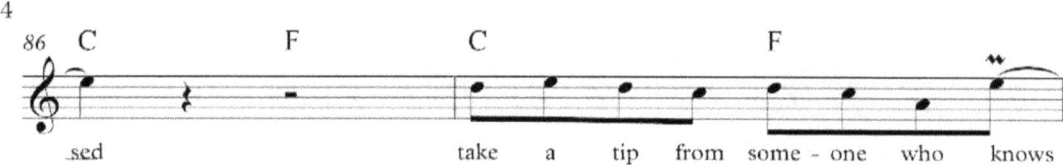
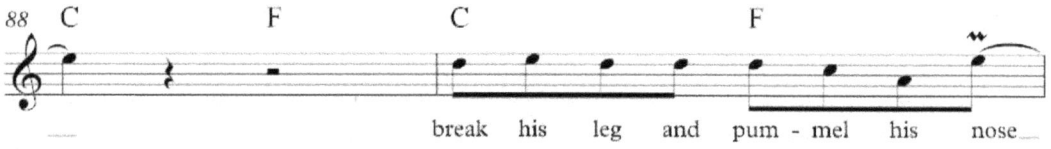
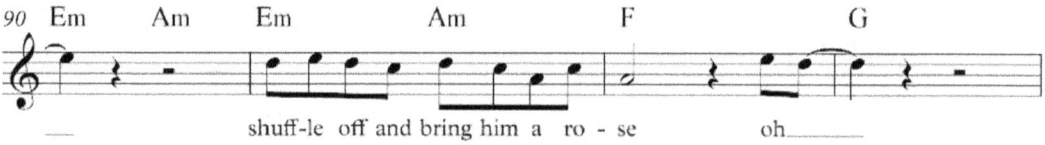
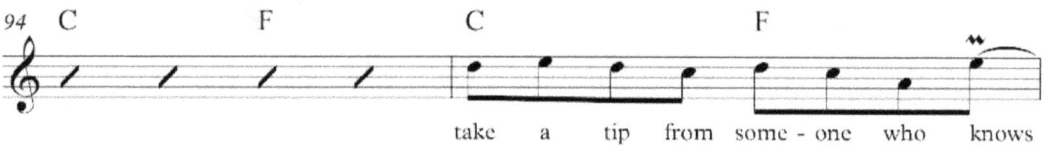
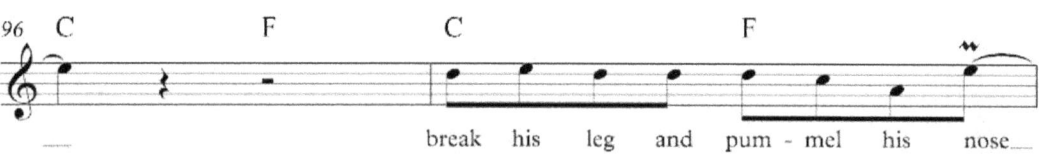
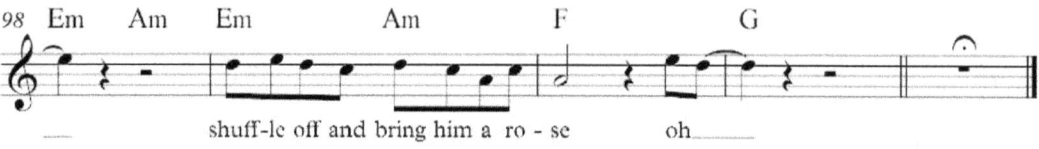

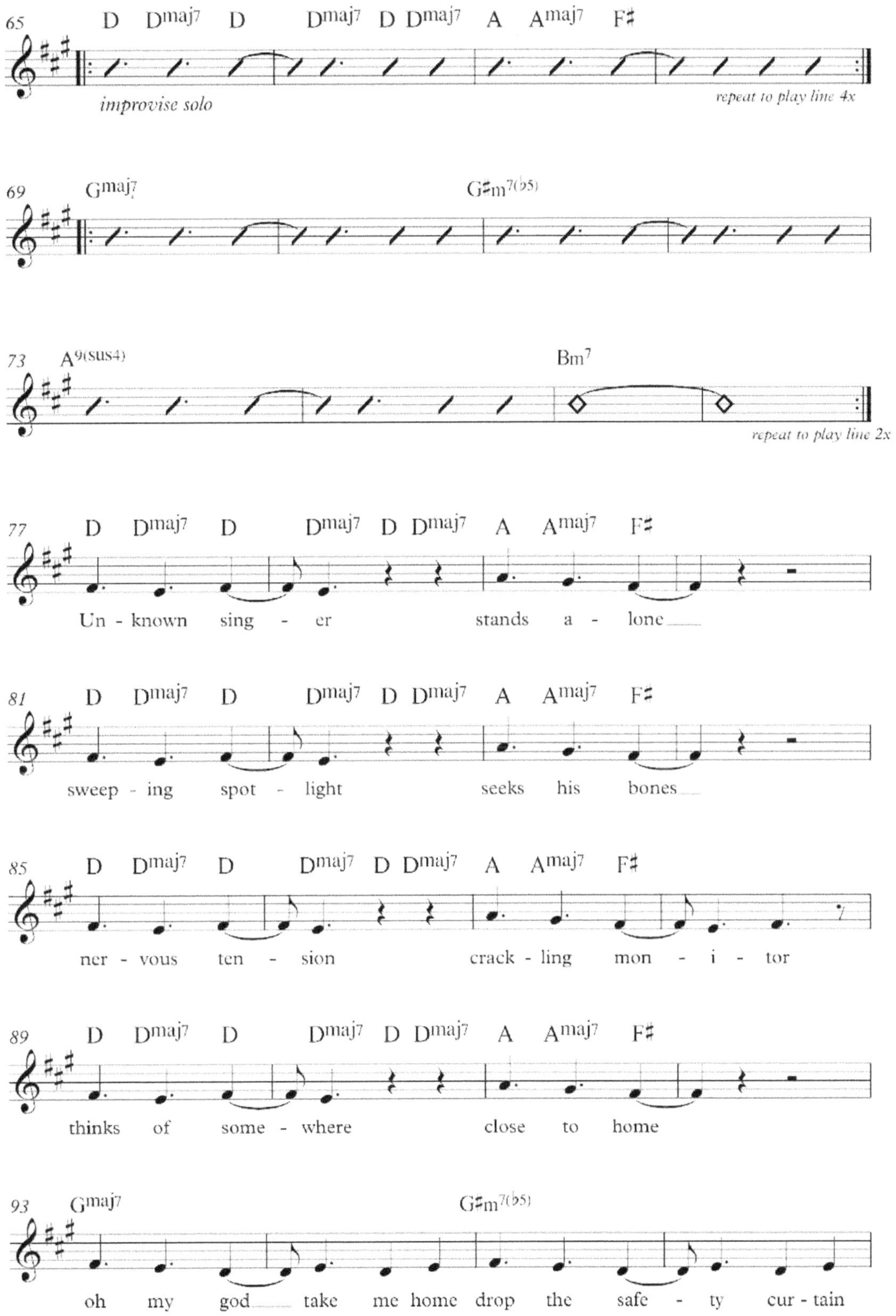
65 D Dmaj7 D Dmaj7 D Dmaj7 A Amaj7 F♯
improvise solo
repeat to play line 4x
69 Gmaj7 G♯m7(♭5)
73 A9(sus4) Bm7
repeat to play line 2x
77 D Dmaj7 D Dmaj7 D Dmaj7 A Amaj7 F♯
Un - known sing - er stands a - lone
81 D Dmaj7 D Dmaj7 D Dmaj7 A Amaj7 F♯
sweep - ing spot - light seeks his bones
85 D Dmaj7 D Dmaj7 D Dmaj7 A Amaj7 F♯
ner - vous ten - sion crack - ling mon - i - tor
89 D Dmaj7 D Dmaj7 D Dmaj7 A Amaj7 F♯
thinks of some - where close to home
93 Gmaj7 G♯m7(♭5)
oh my god take me home drop the safe - ty cur - tain

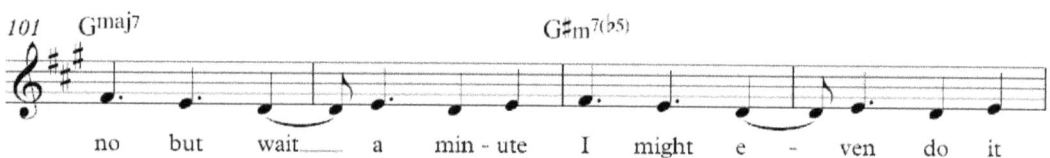

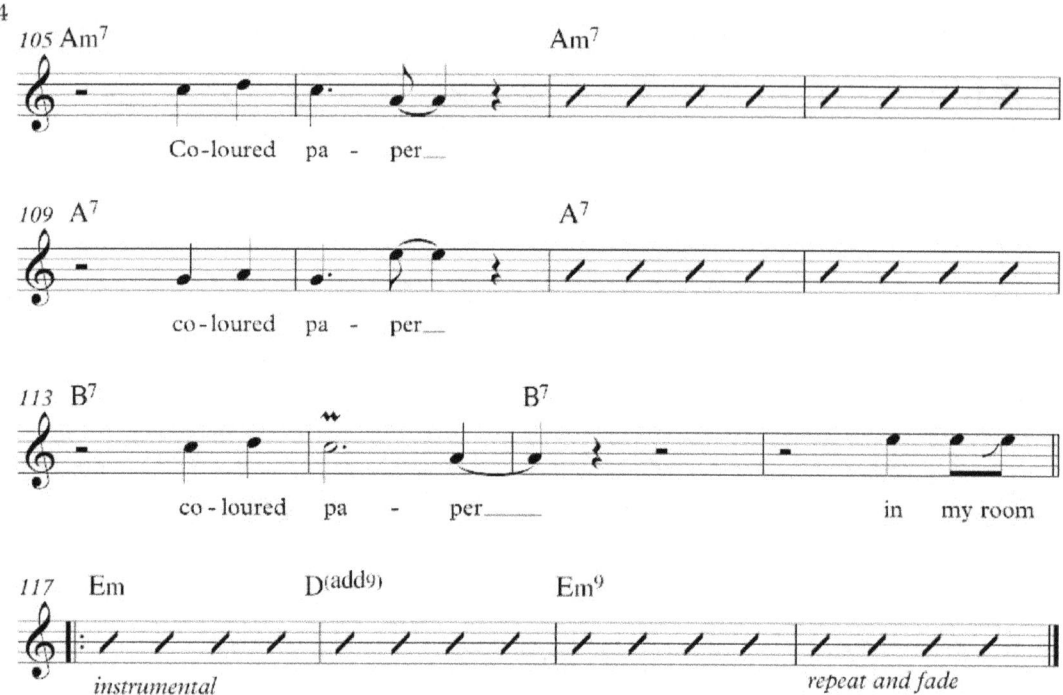

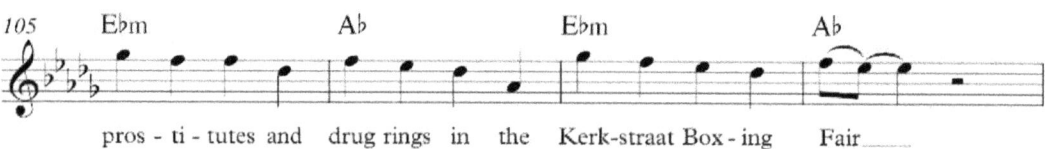
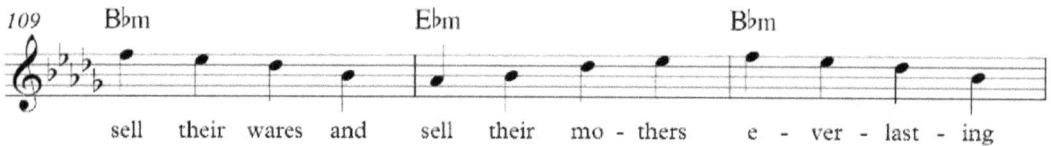
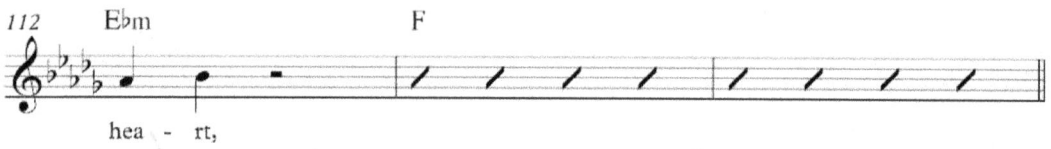
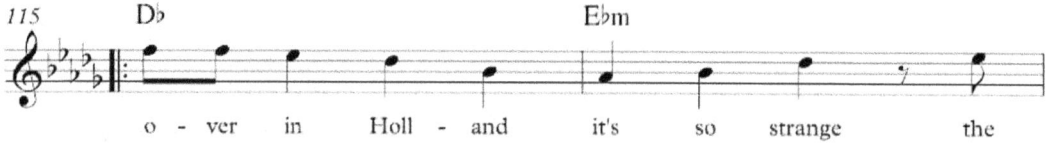
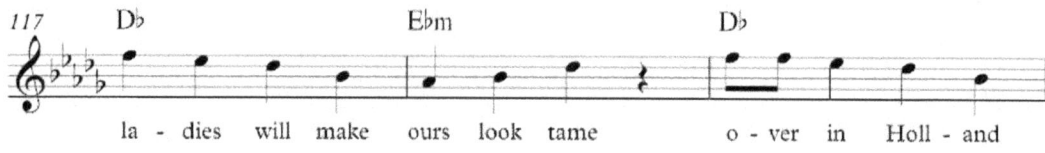
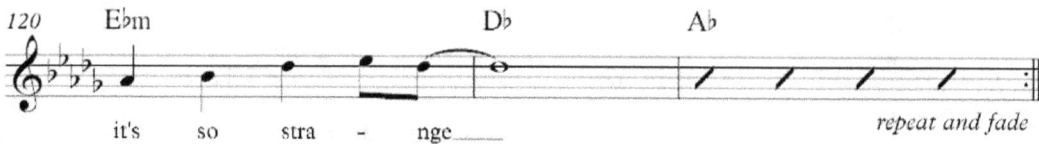

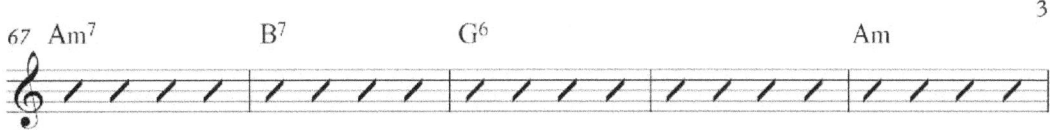
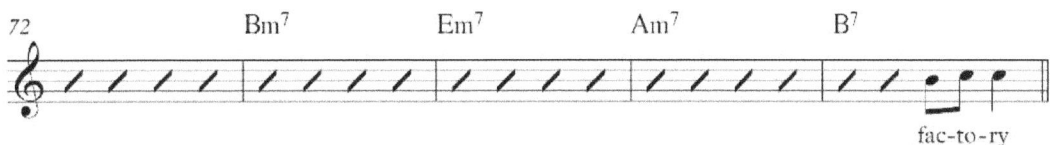

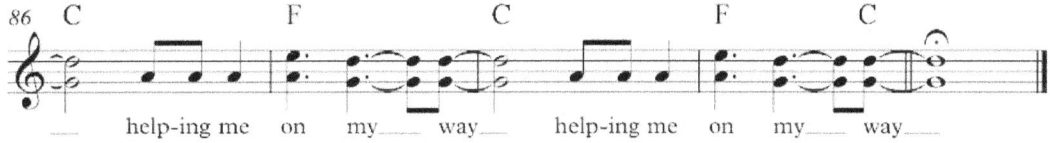

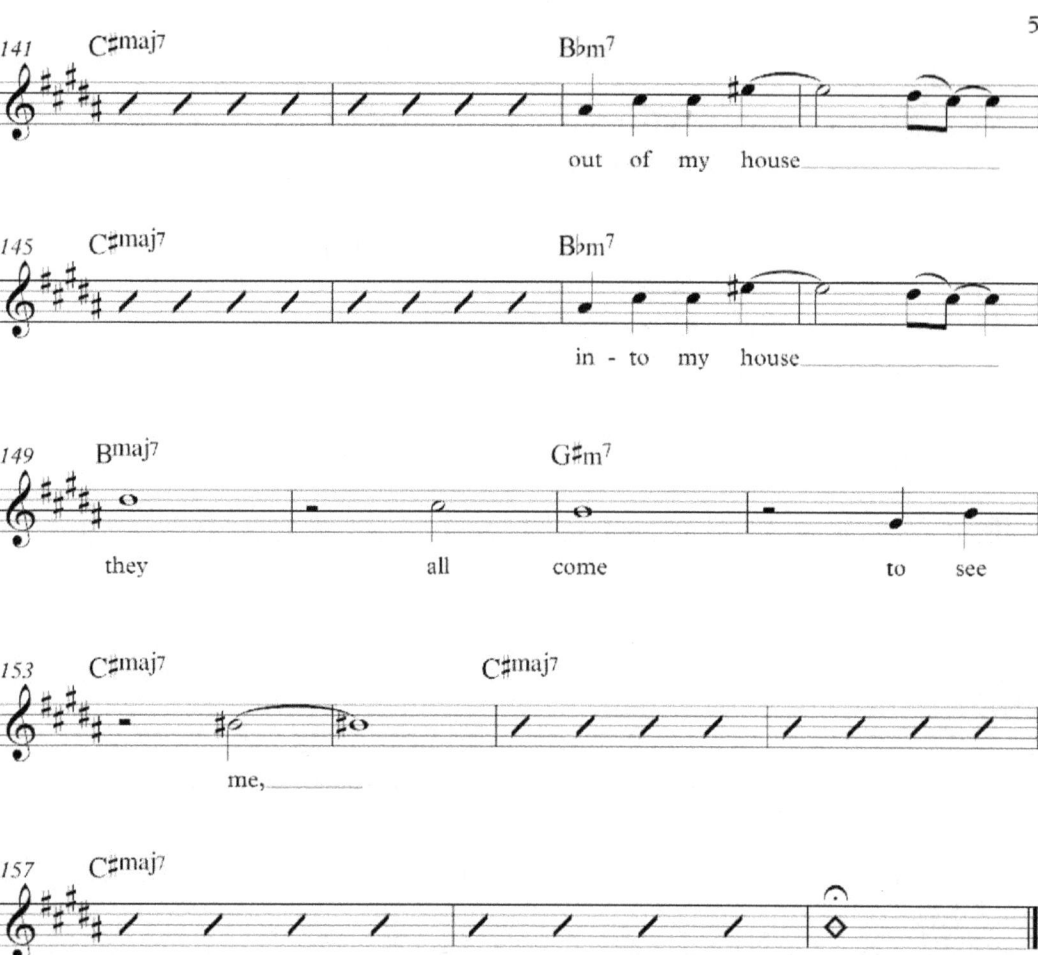

Jehovah's My Witness

41

Klutz and Co.

Words & Music by
B. Perry & G. Steaggles

Lover Cover Girl

Mr. Valentine

Pink Balloons & Frozen Food

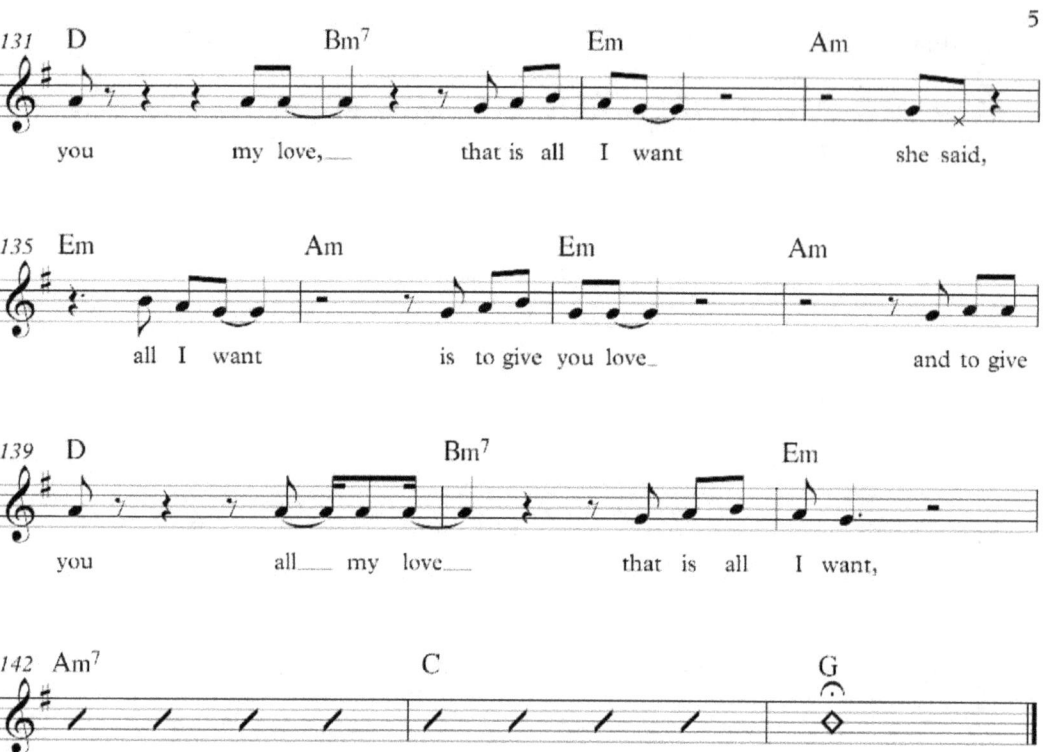

Spy

♩ = 96

Words & Music by
B. Perry & G. Steaggles

While you've got your camera out, take a shot of me
I'm a celebrity I work in a factory and
London Zoo London Zoo at the weekend,
Quick I got my false grin on flick a pic of me
I'm so beautiful, do I astound you?
it's the shape of my nose and my wallet anytime,
anytime, allright

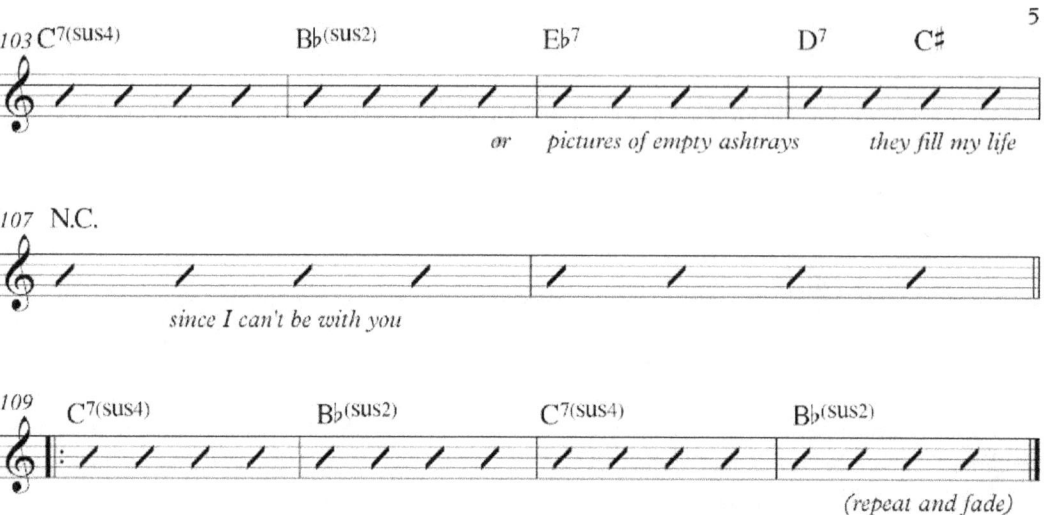

This Is My Night

www.ingramcontent.com/pod-product-compliance
Lightning Source LLC
Chambersburg PA
CBHW080449110426
42743CB00016B/3327